The Coffee Self-Talk
2-Minute
Gratitude Journal

Kristen Helmstetter

*Green
Butterfly
Press*

The Coffee Self-Talk 2-Minute Gratitude Journal

Copyright © 2023 by Kristen Helmstetter

ISBN: 978-1-958625-02-6

v1.1

About the Author

In 2018, Kristen Helmstetter sold everything to travel the world with her husband and daughter. She currently splits her time between the United States and a medieval hilltop town in Italy. She writes romance novels under the pen name Brisa Starr.

Listen to *Coffee Self-Talk with Kristen Helmstetter* wherever you listen to podcasts.

You can also find her on Instagram: Instagram.com/coffeeselftalk

Other Books by Kristen Helmstetter

Coffee Self-Talk

Money Self-Talk

Lipstick Self-Talk

Tea Time Self-Talk

Pillow Self-Talk

Wine Self-Talk

The Coffee Self-Talk Starter Pages

The Coffee Self-Talk Daily Readers (#1 & #2)

The Coffee Self-Talk Guided Journal

Coffee Self-Talk for Dudes

Coffee Self-Talk for Teen Girls

Introduction

Dear Reader,

Welcome to your extra magical life!

By using the *Coffee Self-Talk 2-Minute Gratitude Journal*, you'll take a daily dip into gratitude, where you'll find peace and happiness. It only takes a minute or two to fill out each daily entry, but the results can be profound.

Why is gratitude so amazing?

Gratitude makes you feel as big as the sky. Gratitude makes you feel like everything will always be all right. Gratitude makes you feel magnificent. When you focus on gratitude every day, even if only for a couple of minutes, it helps you live in a gorgeous state of elevated happiness... **all the time.** When you do it regularly, gratitude slowly infuses your core. It becomes your default way of living, like a safe, comfy backdrop to your entire life.

When you create a daily gratitude ritual, your brain begins to naturally see the good things in life. You develop a positive outlook that's always there, humming in the background like a perfectly tuned engine. And this boosts your spirit on a regular basis, raising your baseline of happiness. And you get to enjoy this every day, forever.

Gratitude makes you the best possible you. It inspires you to give more love, more appreciation, more joy, and more energy to things, to give the best of yourself in your life. In turn, you receive all of these things back tenfold, because gratitude is powerfully magnetic.

When you make gratitude a daily little ritual in your life, you will fall asleep with more peace. You'll wake up with a happy grin. You'll fall more in love with life than ever before.

So how do you get there?

The answer is simple: You practice gratitude every day.

Gratitude has enriched my life and taken it to new heights. It has soothed me when I've felt banged-up and bruised by the world. It invigorates me whenever I encounter a rough patch. It has even brought me gushing tears of joy and pure happiness during the most unexpected times. And now that gratitude is in my core—like it's part of my DNA because of my daily practice—it's the greatest *bulletproof-well-being-suit-of-*

armor I could ever wear!

When I live a life of gratitude, everything is always amazing.

So come join me! Join me in a daily gratitude practice and change your life!

All my gratitude to you. Thank you.

P.S. I love hearing from readers! Email me at Kristen@ KristenHelmstetter.com and let me know your experience with this journal or anything that happened to you as you used it.

And be sure to look at the end of this book for a special freebie to add more magic to your life!

KRISTEN HELMSTETTER

How to Use This Journal

In the following pages, you'll find:

1. **Daily entries** – morning and evening sections, where you'll write about the things you're grateful for, what you'll be focusing on, affirmations, and some reflection at the end of the day.

   When you list what you're grateful for, it can be anything. Don't overthink it. You can be grateful for coffee, family, your cat, a sunny day, or feeling great.

2. **Periodic fun exercises** – Lists! (Isn't writing lists so fun?) Specifically, more things you're grateful for (of course), and things you love, which is another great way to feel gratitude and elevate your energy. Again, it's simple... it doesn't require anything special. And that's part of the magic of it. Just write the first things that come to mind.

   You'll also write about your compelling "why?" and do a gratitude doodle! Simply take a minute or two to express feelings of gratitude in any way you want to write, sketch, or draw. You can make a list, draw pictures or squiggles everywhere, or a bunch of hearts and rainbows.

3. **Midway and final check ins** – Halfway through the book and at the end, we'll check in on things. It's a great time to flip through the previous pages and look for any patterns of thoughts, or trends, or gems of insight. Sometimes we don't see the forest through the trees, but once we look at how something unfolds over time, it causes us to see the big picture.

And that's it, my friend!

Using this journal is a simple way to experience a moment of gratitude every day, so you can add more happiness and magic to your life!

GRATITUDE
JOURNAL

Date ____ / ____ / ____   S M T W Th F S

I love doing things that excite me.
I am worthy.

Today, I am grateful for...

Today's Focus or Objectives

Today's Affirmations

How did I do today?

....

....

....

What good things happened today?

....

....

....

What do I look forward to tomorrow?

....

....

....

I spread love everywhere I go,
and if feels so good.

Today, I am grateful for...

_____

_____

_____

_____

Today's Focus or Objectives

_____

_____

_____

Today's Affirmations

_____

_____

_____

EVENING REFLECTION

How did I do today?

What good things happened today?

What do I look forward to tomorrow?

I take care of myself by giving gratitude every day, even if it's only for one thing.

Today, I am grateful for...

_____

_____

_____

_____

Today's Focus or Objectives

_____

_____

_____

Today's Affirmations

_____

_____

_____

EVENING REFLECTION

How did I do today?

....

....

....

What good things happened today?

....

....

....

What do I look forward to tomorrow?

....

....

....

I have grit. I'm grateful for grit.
I dig deep and work hard and smart.

Today, I am grateful for...

_____

_____

_____

_____

Today's Focus or Objectives

_____

_____

_____

Today's Affirmations

_____

_____

_____

EVENING REFLECTION

How did I do today?

....

....

....

What good things happened today?

....

....

....

....

What do I look forward to tomorrow?

....

....

....

Date ____ / ____ / ____   S M T W Th F S

I love being creative.
Thank you! Thank you!

Today, I am grateful for...

Today's Focus or Objectives

Today's Affirmations

EVENING REFLECTION

How did I do today?

....

....

....

What good things happened today?

....

....

....

What do I look forward to tomorrow?

....

....

....

Date ____ / ____ / ____   S   M   T   W   Th   F   S

I'm a great listener,
and I love this about me.

Today, I am grateful for...

_____

_____

_____

_____

Today's Focus or Objectives

_____

_____

_____

Today's Affirmations

_____

_____

_____

EVENING REFLECTION

How did I do today?

What good things happened today?

What do I look forward to tomorrow?

Date ____ / ____ / ____   S   M   T   W   Th   F   S

I love my friends, and I'm grateful for them. Thank you.

Today, I am grateful for...

Today's Focus or Objectives

Today's Affirmations

EVENING REFLECTION

How did I do today?

What good things happened today?

What do I look forward to tomorrow?

I am safe.
My heart is safe. Thank you.

Today, I am grateful for...

_____

_____

_____

Today's Focus or Objectives

_____

_____

Today's Affirmations

_____

_____

_____

EVENING REFLECTION

How did I do today?

....

....

....

What good things happened today?

....

....

....

What do I look forward to tomorrow?

....

....

....

There is no one else in the world like me.
I'm grateful for my uniqueness.

Today, I am grateful for...

Today's Focus or Objectives

Today's Affirmations

EVENING REFLECTION

How did I do today?

....

....

....

What good things happened today?

....

....

....

What do I look forward to tomorrow?

....

....

....

*I'm grateful to be living a completely
new life of my design. Thank you!*

Today, I am grateful for...

_____

_____

_____

_____

Today's Focus or Objectives

_____

_____

_____

Today's Affirmations

_____

_____

_____

EVENING REFLECTION

How did I do today?

....

....

....

What good things happened today?

....

....

....

What do I look forward to tomorrow?

....

....

....

I am full of optimism, and I'm passionate about my destiny.

Today, I am grateful for...

_____

_____

_____

_____

Today's Focus or Objectives

_____

_____

_____

Today's Affirmations

_____

_____

_____

EVENING REFLECTION

How did I do today?

What good things happened today?

What do I look forward to tomorrow?

I believe in me. I just open my heart and connect to this magnificent world.

Today, I am grateful for...

Today's Focus or Objectives

Today's Affirmations

EVENING REFLECTION

How did I do today?

....

....

....

What good things happened today?

....

....

....

What do I look forward to tomorrow?

....

....

....

Date _____ / _____ / _____   S   M   T   W   Th   F   S

Every time I am grateful for something,
I'm telling life, "Yes! More of this!"

Today, I am grateful for...

Today's Focus or Objectives

Today's Affirmations

EVENING REFLECTION

How did I do today?

_____

_____

_____

What good things happened today?

_____

_____

_____

_____

What do I look forward to tomorrow?

_____

_____

_____

Date ____ / ____ / ____   S   M   T   W   Th   F   S

I am grateful for all the smiles coming my way today. Thank you!

Today, I am grateful for...

_____

_____

_____

_____

Today's Focus or Objectives

_____

_____

_____

Today's Affirmations

_____

_____

_____

EVENING REFLECTION

How did I do today?

....

....

....

What good things happened today?

....

....

....

What do I look forward to tomorrow?

....

....

....

Date ____ / ____ / ____   S M T W Th F S

I am overflowing with gratitude for the abundance and prosperity in my life.

Today, I am grateful for...

_____

_____

_____

_____

Today's Focus or Objectives

_____

_____

_____

Today's Affirmations

_____

_____

_____

EVENING REFLECTION

How did I do today?

....

....

....

What good things happened today?

....

....

....

What do I look forward to tomorrow?

....

....

....

Date ____ / ____ / ____   S   M   T   W   Th   F   S

I'm free as a bird, ready to take flight
because my kind heart is expansive.

Today, I am grateful for...

Today's Focus or Objectives

Today's Affirmations

EVENING REFLECTION

How did I do today?

....

....

....

What good things happened today?

....

....

....

What do I look forward to tomorrow?

....

....

....

I love being generous with others.
It makes the world a better place.

Today, I am grateful for...

Today's Focus or Objectives

Today's Affirmations

EVENING REFLECTION

How did I do today?

....

....

....

What good things happened today?

....

....

....

What do I look forward to tomorrow?

....

....

....

I put out high-vibes day and night.
This attracts that which I desire.

Today, I am grateful for...

_____

_____

_____

_____

Today's Focus or Objectives

_____

_____

_____

Today's Affirmations

_____

_____

_____

EVENING REFLECTION

How did I do today?

....

....

....

What good things happened today?

....

....

....

What do I look forward to tomorrow?

....

....

....

Date ____ / ____ / ____   S M T W Th F S

*I'm in awe of nature
and the world around me.*

Today, I am grateful for...

Today's Focus or Objectives

Today's Affirmations

EVENING REFLECTION

How did I do today?

....

....

....

What good things happened today?

....

....

....

What do I look forward to tomorrow?

....

....

....

My life is magnificent because
I make it so. I am in charge.

Today, I am grateful for...

Today's Focus or Objectives

Today's Affirmations

EVENING REFLECTION

How did I do today?

What good things happened today?

What do I look forward to tomorrow?

Date ____ / ____ / ____   S   M   T   W   Th   F   S

I am open to receive—yes!
Thank you!

Today, I am grateful for...

Today's Focus or Objectives

Today's Affirmations

How did I do today?

....

....

....

What good things happened today?

....

....

....

....

What do I look forward to tomorrow?

....

....

....

Date ____ / ____ / ____   S   M   T   W   Th   F   S

I have purpose in my life.
I have unlimited potential!

Today, I am grateful for...

_____

_____

_____

_____

Today's Focus or Objectives

_____

_____

_____

Today's Affirmations

_____

_____

_____

EVENING REFLECTION

How did I do today?

....

....

....

What good things happened today?

....

....

....

What do I look forward to tomorrow?

....

....

....

Date ____ / ____ / ____   S   M   T   W   Th   F   S

I encourage myself every day,
*because I can do it. I **am** doing it!*

Today, I am grateful for...

_____

_____

_____

_____

Today's Focus or Objectives

_____

_____

_____

Today's Affirmations

_____

_____

_____

EVENING REFLECTION

How did I do today?

....

....

....

What good things happened today?

....

....

....

What do I look forward to tomorrow?

....

....

....

I remember things easily. My brain is magnificent. My memory is phenomenal.

Today, I am grateful for...

_____

_____

_____

Today's Focus or Objectives

_____

_____

Today's Affirmations

_____

_____

_____

EVENING REFLECTION

How did I do today?

_____

_____

_____

What good things happened today?

_____

_____

_____

What do I look forward to tomorrow?

_____

_____

_____

Date ____ / ____ / ____   S   M   T   W   Th   F   S

I love meeting new people.
I love listening to others and learning.

Today, I am grateful for...

_____

_____

_____

_____

Today's Focus or Objectives

_____

_____

_____

Today's Affirmations

_____

_____

_____

EVENING REFLECTION

How did I do today?

....

....

....

What good things happened today?

....

....

....

What do I look forward to tomorrow?

....

....

....

I'M SO GRATEFUL FOR...

1. ....
2. ....
3. ....
4. ....
5. ....
6. ....
7. ....
8. ....
9. ....
10. ....
11. ....
12. ....
13. ....
14. ....
15. ....

I LOVE...

1. ....
2. ....
3. ....
4. ....
5. ....
6. ....
7. ....
8. ....
9. ....
10. ....
11. ....
12. ....
13. ....
14. ....
15. ....

MY COMPELLING "WHY"

1. I am so happy and grateful for...

    ....

    because ....

    ....

2. I am so happy and grateful for...

    ....

    because ....

    ....

3. I am so happy and grateful for...

    ....

    because ....

    ....

GRATITUDE DOODLE

Date ____ / ____ / ____   S   M   T   W   Th   F   S

I am renewed. I am revitalized. I am grateful for another amazing day.

Today, I am grateful for...

Today's Focus or Objectives

Today's Affirmations

EVENING REFLECTION

How did I do today?

....

....

....

What good things happened today?

....

....

....

What do I look forward to tomorrow?

....

....

....

Date ____ / ____ / ____   S   M   T   W   Th   F   S

I feel uplifted right here and right now,
because I'm taking care of me.

Today, I am grateful for...

Today's Focus or Objectives

Today's Affirmations

EVENING REFLECTION

How did I do today?

....

....

....

What good things happened today?

....

....

....

What do I look forward to tomorrow?

....

....

....

Date ____ / ____ / ____   S   M   T   W   Th   F   S

I'm having an awesome day today!
Thank you!

Today, I am grateful for...

Today's Focus or Objectives

Today's Affirmations

EVENING REFLECTION

How did I do today?

....

....

....

What good things happened today?

....

....

....

What do I look forward to tomorrow?

....

....

....

Date ____ / ____ / ____   S   M   T   W   Th   F   S

I LOVE feeling so awesome!
YESSS!

Today, I am grateful for...

_____

_____

_____

_____

Today's Focus or Objectives

_____

_____

_____

Today's Affirmations

_____

_____

_____

EVENING REFLECTION

How did I do today?

What good things happened today?

What do I look forward to tomorrow?

*My worthiness is the foundation
of my life, my soul, my being.*

Today, I am grateful for...

Today's Focus or Objectives

Today's Affirmations

EVENING REFLECTION

How did I do today?

....

....

....

What good things happened today?

....

....

....

What do I look forward to tomorrow?

....

....

....

*I am full of power. I can do anything
I want. I step into my life now.*

Today, I am grateful for...

_____

_____

_____

_____

Today's Focus or Objectives

_____

_____

_____

Today's Affirmations

_____

_____

_____

EVENING REFLECTION

How did I do today?

What good things happened today?

What do I look forward to tomorrow?

I raise my flag to the sky. I'm here.
I'm ready. Self-love is my passion cry!

Today, I am grateful for...

_____

_____

_____

_____

Today's Focus or Objectives

_____

_____

_____

Today's Affirmations

_____

_____

_____

EVENING REFLECTION

How did I do today?

....

....

....

What good things happened today?

....

....

....

What do I look forward to tomorrow?

....

....

....

Date ____ / ____ / ____   S   M   T   W   Th   F   S

I'm on the ride of my life,
and I appreciate every breath.

Today, I am grateful for...

....

....

....

....

Today's Focus or Objectives

....

....

....

Today's Affirmations

....

....

....

EVENING REFLECTION

How did I do today?

_____

_____

_____

What good things happened today?

_____

_____

_____

_____

What do I look forward to tomorrow?

_____

_____

_____

Date ____ / ____ / ____   S   M   T   W   Th   F   S

I wake up every morning with warmth
and gratitude fueling my day.

Today, I am grateful for...

Today's Focus or Objectives

Today's Affirmations

How did I do today?

What good things happened today?

What do I look forward to tomorrow?

Date _____ / _____ / _____   S   M   T   W   Th   F   S

I am blessed with prosperity,
abundance, and opportunities.

Today, I am grateful for...

_____

_____

_____

_____

Today's Focus or Objectives

_____

_____

_____

Today's Affirmations

_____

_____

_____

EVENING REFLECTION

How did I do today?

_____

_____

_____

What good things happened today?

_____

_____

_____

What do I look forward to tomorrow?

_____

_____

_____

Date ____ / ____ / ____   S   M   T   W   Th   F   S

I am in the right place at the right time,
doing the right thing. Thank you.

Today, I am grateful for...

_____

_____

_____

_____

Today's Focus or Objectives

_____

_____

Today's Affirmations

_____

_____

_____

EVENING REFLECTION

How did I do today?

What good things happened today?

What do I look forward to tomorrow?

*My body hums with life,
and I feel young and vibrant.*

Today, I am grateful for...

Today's Focus or Objectives

Today's Affirmations

EVENING REFLECTION

How did I do today?

What good things happened today?

What do I look forward to tomorrow?

MIDPOINT CHECK-IN

1. How does it feel to give gratitude every day? Is it easy? Is it ever difficult? If so, how can I make it easier?

   ....

   ....

   ....

   ....

2. What do I find myself giving thanks for the most?

   ....

   ....

3. As I look back through this journal, have my thoughts on gratitude changed? Are there any patterns over time?

   ....

   ....

MIDPOINT CHECK-IN

4. How can I use gratitude to make every day better?

_____

_____

_____

_____

_____

5. Are there things I want to change but haven't yet?
   If so, what holds me back? How can I make changes
   going forward?

_____

_____

_____

_____

_____

_____

Date ____ / ____ / ____   S   M   T   W   Th   F   S

I have integrity and I show up,
ready to prosper every day.

Today, I am grateful for...

_____

_____

_____

_____

Today's Focus or Objectives

_____

_____

_____

Today's Affirmations

_____

_____

_____

EVENING REFLECTION

How did I do today?

....

....

....

What good things happened today?

....

....

....

What do I look forward to tomorrow?

....

....

....

Date ____ / ____ / ____   S   M   T   W   Th   F   S

I own my life.
Yeah baby!

Today, I am grateful for...

_____

_____

_____

_____

Today's Focus or Objectives

_____

_____

_____

Today's Affirmations

_____

_____

_____

EVENING REFLECTION

How did I do today?

....

....

....

What good things happened today?

....

....

....

What do I look forward to tomorrow?

....

....

....

Date ____ / ____ / ____   S M T W Th F S

I expect achievement. I expect to succeed.
Of course! Thank you!

Today, I am grateful for...

_____

_____

_____

_____

Today's Focus or Objectives

_____

_____

_____

Today's Affirmations

_____

_____

_____

EVENING REFLECTION

How did I do today?

....

....

....

What good things happened today?

....

....

....

What do I look forward to tomorrow?

....

....

....

*I have a foundation of gratitude
and calm. It feels perfect.*

Today, I am grateful for...

_____

_____

_____

_____

Today's Focus or Objectives

_____

_____

_____

Today's Affirmations

_____

_____

_____

EVENING REFLECTION

How did I do today?

_____

_____

_____

What good things happened today?

_____

_____

_____

What do I look forward to tomorrow?

_____

_____

_____

I am curious, happy, open-minded,
and interested in what I am doing.

Today, I am grateful for...

_____

_____

_____

Today's Focus or Objectives

_____

_____

Today's Affirmations

_____

_____

_____

EVENING REFLECTION

How did I do today?

....

....

....

What good things happened today?

....

....

....

What do I look forward to tomorrow?

....

....

....

Life is a party! My life is a party!
I love life!

Today, I am grateful for...

_____

_____

_____

_____

Today's Focus or Objectives

_____

_____

_____

Today's Affirmations

_____

_____

_____

EVENING REFLECTION

How did I do today?

What good things happened today?

What do I look forward to tomorrow?

Date ____ / ____ / ____   S   M   T   W   Th   F   S

It's a good, great, wonderful, mighty spectacular day! Thank you!

Today, I am grateful for...

_____

_____

_____

_____

Today's Focus or Objectives

_____

_____

_____

Today's Affirmations

_____

_____

_____

How did I do today?

....

....

....

What good things happened today?

....

....

....

What do I look forward to tomorrow?

....

....

....

I attract happy people, because my heart is filled with love.

Today, I am grateful for...

_____

_____

_____

_____

Today's Focus or Objectives

_____

_____

_____

Today's Affirmations

_____

_____

_____

EVENING REFLECTION

How did I do today?

What good things happened today?

What do I look forward to tomorrow?

Date ____ / ____ / ____   S   M   T   W   Th   F   S

*I wake up filled with
sunshine in my soul.*

Today, I am grateful for...

_____

_____

_____

_____

Today's Focus or Objectives

_____

_____

_____

Today's Affirmations

_____

_____

_____

EVENING REFLECTION

How did I do today?

....

....

....

What good things happened today?

....

....

....

What do I look forward to tomorrow?

....

....

....

I flipped the switch to feeling abundance.
I now glow with this knowing.

Today, I am grateful for...

Today's Focus or Objectives

Today's Affirmations

EVENING REFLECTION

How did I do today?

....

....

....

What good things happened today?

....

....

....

What do I look forward to tomorrow?

....

....

....

I'm a great best friend to myself.
I'm gentle with me. I love me.

Today, I am grateful for...

....

....

....

....

Today's Focus or Objectives

....

....

....

Today's Affirmations

....

....

....

EVENING REFLECTION

How did I do today?

....

....

....

What good things happened today?

....

....

....

What do I look forward to tomorrow?

....

....

....

I love caring for myself.
It's fundamental to living my best life.

Today, I am grateful for...

Today's Focus or Objectives

Today's Affirmations

EVENING REFLECTION

How did I do today?

....

....

....

What good things happened today?

....

....

....

What do I look forward to tomorrow?

....

....

....

Date ____ / ____ / ____   S   M   T   W   Th   F   S

I control my attitude. I control my effort.
I'm in charge of my life.

Today, I am grateful for...

_____

_____

_____

_____

Today's Focus or Objectives

_____

_____

_____

Today's Affirmations

_____

_____

_____

EVENING REFLECTION

How did I do today?

What good things happened today?

What do I look forward to tomorrow?

I'M SO GRATEFUL FOR...

1. ....
2. ....
3. ....
4. ....
5. ....
6. ....
7. ....
8. ....
9. ....
10. ....
11. ....
12. ....
13. ....
14. ....
15. ....

I LOVE...

1. ....

2. ....

3. ....

4. ....

5. ....

6. ....

7. ....

8. ....

9. ....

10. ....

11. ....

12. ....

13. ....

14. ....

15. ....

MY COMPELLING "WHY"

1. I am so happy and grateful for...

   ....

   because ....

   ....

2. I am so happy and grateful for...

   ....

   because ....

   ....

3. I am so happy and grateful for...

   ....

   because ....

   ....

GRATITUDE DOODLE

Date ____ / ____ / ____   S M T W Th F S

I can do anything.
Of course I can!

Today, I am grateful for...

_____

_____

_____

_____

Today's Focus or Objectives

_____

_____

Today's Affirmations

_____

_____

_____

EVENING REFLECTION

How did I do today?

....

....

....

What good things happened today?

....

....

....

What do I look forward to tomorrow?

....

....

....

I love moving, stretching, and strengthening my body every day.

Today, I am grateful for...

Today's Focus or Objectives

Today's Affirmations

EVENING REFLECTION

How did I do today?

What good things happened today?

What do I look forward to tomorrow?

Date ____ / ____ / ____   S M T W Th F S

Only greatness lies before me.
I am ready to receive.

Today, I am grateful for...

_____

_____

_____

_____

Today's Focus or Objectives

_____

_____

_____

Today's Affirmations

_____

_____

_____

EVENING REFLECTION

How did I do today?

....

....

....

What good things happened today?

....

....

....

What do I look forward to tomorrow?

....

....

....

I let go with ease, and I easily attract the best things.

Today, I am grateful for...

Today's Focus or Objectives

Today's Affirmations

EVENING REFLECTION

How did I do today?

....

....

....

What good things happened today?

....

....

....

What do I look forward to tomorrow?

....

....

....

Date ____ / ____ / ____   S   M   T   W   Th   F   S

My life gets more fabulous
each and every day. Thank you!

Today, I am grateful for...

_____

_____

_____

_____

Today's Focus or Objectives

_____

_____

_____

Today's Affirmations

_____

_____

_____

EVENING REFLECTION

How did I do today?

....

....

....

What good things happened today?

....

....

....

What do I look forward to tomorrow?

....

....

....

Date ____ / ____ / ____   S   M   T   W   Th   F   S

I am worthy and brave.
I am wildly resourceful.

Today, I am grateful for...

_____

_____

_____

_____

Today's Focus or Objectives

_____

_____

_____

Today's Affirmations

_____

_____

_____

EVENING REFLECTION

How did I do today?

....

....

....

What good things happened today?

....

....

....

....

What do I look forward to tomorrow?

....

....

....

*I release the need for approval
from others. I let go with ease.*

Today, I am grateful for...

_____

_____

_____

_____

Today's Focus or Objectives

_____

_____

_____

Today's Affirmations

_____

_____

_____

EVENING REFLECTION

How did I do today?

....

....

....

What good things happened today?

....

....

....

....

What do I look forward to tomorrow?

....

....

....

Date ____ / ____ / ____   S   M   T   W   Th   F   S

*I rest easy knowing the perfect solutions
are coming to me right now. Thank you.*

Today, I am grateful for...

_____

_____

_____

_____

Today's Focus or Objectives

_____

_____

_____

Today's Affirmations

_____

_____

_____

EVENING REFLECTION

How did I do today?

....

....

....

What good things happened today?

....

....

....

What do I look forward to tomorrow?

....

....

....

Date _____ / _____ / _____   S   M   T   W   Th   F   S

I encourage myself every day, because
I can do it. I AM doing it. Yes!

Today, I am grateful for...

Today's Focus or Objectives

Today's Affirmations

EVENING REFLECTION

How did I do today?

....
....
....

What good things happened today?

....
....
....

What do I look forward to tomorrow?

....
....
....

Date ____ / ____ / ____   S   M   T   W   Th   F   S

Things always align perfectly for me
in the best possible ways.

Today, I am grateful for...

_____

_____

_____

_____

Today's Focus or Objectives

_____

_____

_____

Today's Affirmations

_____

_____

EVENING REFLECTION

How did I do today?

....

....

....

What good things happened today?

....

....

....

What do I look forward to tomorrow?

....

....

....

Date ____ / ____ / ____   S M T W Th F S

I make smart and healthy choices,
and these choices lead to a better life.

Today, I am grateful for...

Today's Focus or Objectives

Today's Affirmations

EVENING REFLECTION

How did I do today?

....

....

What good things happened today?

....

....

....

What do I look forward to tomorrow?

....

....

....

Date ____ / ____ / ____   S M T W Th F S

I am happy wherever I am, glittering
with gratitude. Thank you, Life.

Today, I am grateful for...

Today's Focus or Objectives

Today's Affirmations

EVENING REFLECTION

How did I do today?

....

....

....

What good things happened today?

....

....

....

....

What do I look forward to tomorrow?

....

....

....

Date ____ / ____ / ____   S   M   T   W   Th   F   S

I feel completely at peace.
It's all around me.

Today, I am grateful for...

_____

_____

_____

Today's Focus or Objectives

_____

_____

Today's Affirmations

_____

_____

_____

EVENING REFLECTION

How did I do today?

....

....

....

What good things happened today?

....

....

....

What do I look forward to tomorrow?

....

....

....

Today is my day.
I am the master of my mind.

Today, I am grateful for...

_____

_____

_____

_____

Today's Focus or Objectives

_____

_____

_____

Today's Affirmations

_____

_____

_____

EVENING REFLECTION

How did I do today?

....

....

....

What good things happened today?

....

....

....

What do I look forward to tomorrow?

....

....

....

Date ____ / ____ / ____   S   M   T   W   Th   F   S

I am meant for great things.
I am here for a reason.

Today, I am grateful for...

_____

_____

_____

_____

Today's Focus or Objectives

_____

_____

_____

Today's Affirmations

_____

_____

_____

EVENING REFLECTION

How did I do today?

....

....

....

What good things happened today?

....

....

....

What do I look forward to tomorrow?

....

....

....

I am grateful for knowing the power and magic of my own mind.

Today, I am grateful for...

_____

_____

_____

_____

Today's Focus or Objectives

_____

_____

_____

Today's Affirmations

_____

_____

_____

EVENING REFLECTION

How did I do today?

....

....

....

What good things happened today?

....

....

....

....

What do I look forward to tomorrow?

....

....

....

I make great choices, and my brain listens.
Thank you, brain!

Today, I am grateful for...

_____

_____

_____

_____

Today's Focus or Objectives

_____

_____

_____

Today's Affirmations

_____

_____

_____

EVENING REFLECTION

How did I do today?

What good things happened today?

What do I look forward to tomorrow?

*I awaken my own glittering fire
inside me. I'm ready for anything!*

Today, I am grateful for...

Today's Focus or Objectives

Today's Affirmations

EVENING REFLECTION

How did I do today?

....

....

....

What good things happened today?

....

....

....

What do I look forward to tomorrow?

....

....

....

Date ____ / ____ / ____   S   M   T   W   Th   F   S

I show up to my life, because
my life is meaningful.

Today, I am grateful for...

Today's Focus or Objectives

Today's Affirmations

EVENING REFLECTION

How did I do today?

_____

_____

_____

What good things happened today?

_____

_____

_____

What do I look forward to tomorrow?

_____

_____

_____

I see my incredible potential,
and I tap into this every single day.

Today, I am grateful for...

Today's Focus or Objectives

Today's Affirmations

EVENING REFLECTION

How did I do today?

_____

_____

_____

What good things happened today?

_____

_____

_____

What do I look forward to tomorrow?

_____

_____

_____

Date ____ / ____ / ____   S   M   T   W   Th   F   S

My bright future is all up to me.
I call the shots!

Today, I am grateful for...

_____

_____

_____

_____

Today's Focus or Objectives

_____

_____

_____

Today's Affirmations

_____

_____

_____

EVENING REFLECTION

How did I do today?

_____

_____

_____

What good things happened today?

_____

_____

_____

What do I look forward to tomorrow?

_____

_____

_____

*I believe in my incredible
dreams, desires, and goals.*

Today, I am grateful for...

Today's Focus or Objectives

Today's Affirmations

EVENING REFLECTION

How did I do today?

What good things happened today?

What do I look forward to tomorrow?

When I direct my thoughts, it directs my focus, and this changes my life.

Today, I am grateful for...

_____

_____

_____

_____

Today's Focus or Objectives

_____

_____

_____

Today's Affirmations

_____

_____

_____

EVENING REFLECTION

How did I do today?

What good things happened today?

What do I look forward to tomorrow?

*I look around today, and I see
the beauty everywhere. Thank you.*

Today, I am grateful for...

_____

_____

_____

_____

Today's Focus or Objectives

_____

_____

_____

Today's Affirmations

_____

_____

_____

EVENING REFLECTION

How did I do today?

....

....

....

What good things happened today?

....

....

....

What do I look forward to tomorrow?

....

....

....

Date ____ / ____ / ____   S   M   T   W   Th   F   S

I want a magnificent life,
so I think magnificent thoughts.

Today, I am grateful for...

Today's Focus or Objectives

Today's Affirmations

EVENING REFLECTION

How did I do today?

....

....

....

What good things happened today?

....

....

....

What do I look forward to tomorrow?

....

....

....

FINAL CHECK-IN

1. How does it feel to give gratitude every day? Is it easy? Is it ever difficult? If so, how can I make it easier?

2. What do I find myself giving thanks for the most?

3. As I look back through this journal, have my thoughts on gratitude changed? Are there any patterns over time?

FINAL CHECK-IN

4. How can I use gratitude to make every day better?

_____

_____

_____

_____

_____

5. Are there things I want to change but haven't yet?
   If so, what holds me back? How can I make changes
   going forward?

_____

_____

_____

_____

_____

KRISTEN HELMSTETTER

Conclusion

Thank you for doing your daily *Coffee Self-Talk Gratitude* journaling. It's such a wonderful way to add an extra layer of sparkle to your regular Coffee Self-Talk routine.

I love to hear from my readers. You can reach me at:

Kristen@KristenHelmstetter.com

FREE GIFT: For a free recorded *Gratitude* MP3 audio script, email me and ask for the "Gratitude Journal Goodies."

Podcast

You can listen to me on my podcast, *Coffee Self-Talk with Kristen Helmstetter,* wherever you listen to podcasts.

I have a HUGE favor to ask of you...

If you would help me, I'd greatly appreciate it. If you enjoyed this book, I'd love it if you would leave a review for it on Amazon. Reviews are incredibly important for authors, and I'd be extremely grateful if you would write one!

What's Next?

Here are a few more members of the Coffee Self-Talk family:

International Bestseller – Over 150,000 Copies Sold

Coffee Self-Talk:
5 Minutes a Day to Start Living Your Magical Life

Coffee Self-Talk is a powerful, life-changing routine that takes only 5 minutes a day. Coffee Self-Talk transforms your life by boosting your self-esteem, filling you with happiness, and helping you attract the magical life you dream of living. All this, with your next cup of coffee.

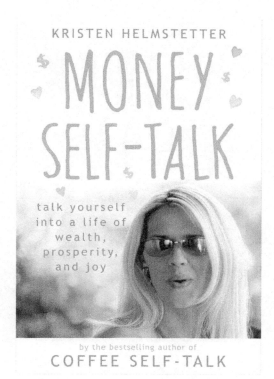

Money Self-Talk:
Talk Yourself Into a Life of Wealth, Prosperity, and Joy

Building wealth requires doing things differently. But where do you start? How do you make the change? How do you overcome a lifetime of bad habits and self-defeating beliefs? The answer is Money Self-Talk, a simple but highly effective tool for rewiring your brain to change your behaviors to create a life of wealth, prosperity, and joy.

Lipstick Self-Talk:
A Radical Little Self-Love Book

It's time to make your dreams come true, but you must start with a *rock-solid foundation of self-love*. Provocative, fun, quirky, and uplifting, *Lipstick Self-Talk* launches you into living your most magical life by teaching you how to *truly love yourself*. Kristen leads you step-by-step with clear insights, sassy words, and poignant stories, showing you how amazing you truly are.

The Coffee Self-Talk Daily Reader #1:
Bite-Sized Nuggets of Magic
to Add to Your Morning Routine

This companion book offers short, daily reads for tips and inspiration. It does not replace your daily Coffee Self-Talk routine. Rather, it's meant to be used each day *after* you do your Coffee Self-Talk.

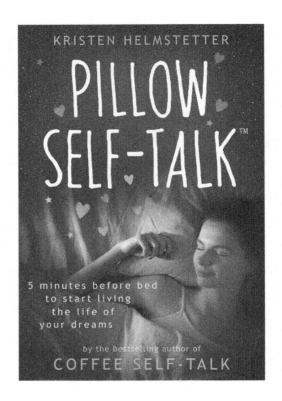

Pillow Self-Talk:
5 Minutes Before Bed to Start Living
the Life of Your Dreams

End your day with a powerful nighttime ritual to help you manifest your dreams, reach your goals, find peace, relaxation, and happiness... all while getting the very *best sleep ever!*

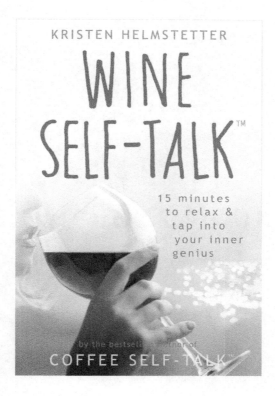

Wine Self-Talk:
15 Minutes to Relax & Tap Into Your Inner Genius

There is a source of sacred wisdom in you. Wine Self-Talk is a simple, delicious ritual to help you relax, unwind, and tap into your inner genius.

The Coffee Self-Talk Guided Journal:
Writing Prompts & Inspiration for Living Your Magical Life

This guided journal keeps you lit up and glowing as you go deeper into your magical Coffee Self-Talk journey. Experience the joy of journaling, mixed with fun exercises, and discover hidden gems about yourself. Get inspired, slash your anxiety, and unleash your amazing, badass self.

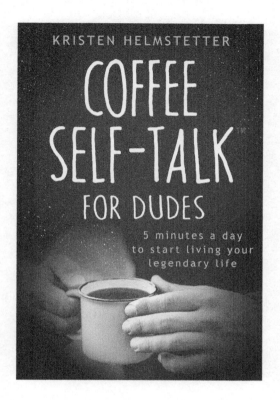

Coffee Self-Talk for Dudes:
5 Minutes a Day to Start Living Your Legendary Life

This is a special edition of *Coffee Self-Talk* that has been edited to be more oriented toward men in the language, examples, and scripts. It is 95% identical to the original Coffee Self-Talk book.

Made in the USA
Monee, IL
19 September 2023